WHAT GETS LOST

WHAT GETS LOST

Poems by Doris Henderson

Best wishes + happy reading —
Doris Henderson

Antrim House
Simsbury, Connecticut

Copyright © 2009 by Doris Henderson

Except for short selections reprinted for purposes of
book review, all reproduction rights are reserved.
Requests for permission to replicate should
be addressed to the publisher.

Library of Congress Control Number: 2009938011

ISBN: 978-0-9823970-0-8

Printed & bound by United Graphics, Inc.

First Edition, 2009

Cover painting by Joseph Farris (www.josephfarris.com)
24" x 30" untitled acrylic

Photograph of author: Truus Teeuwissen

Book Design: Rennie McQuilkin

Antrim House
860.217.0023
AntrimHouse@comcast.net
www.AntrimHouseBooks.com
21 Goodrich Road, Simsbury, CT 06070

Acknowledgments

Grateful acknowledgment to the editors of the following publications in which these poems originally appeared:

BENT PIN QUARTERLY: *She, Mona's Wedding, Structure, Three A.M.*
BLACK RIVER REVIEW: *The Swimmer*
CADUCEUS: *Exiles, Pardon Me, Distances, The Victorian Ladies, Seers, Generosity*
CALLIOPE: *Intruders*
COMMON GROUND REVIEW: *Tiger*
COMSTOCK REVIEW: *Burnings, Connections*
CONNECTICUT RIVER REVIEW: *Cookie Cutters, Patrons, The Lake, Deliverance*
GODDESS RISING: *Renewal*
HIGH TIDE: *Small Boat at Anchor, Seascape*
HOBO JUNGLE: *Kali of the Underground*
THE NEW PRESS: *The Harvest*
NEW VERSE NEWS: *Bomb, Ruminations of an Aging Feminist*
PARTING GIFTS: *Years Ago, Turning, Walking the Planck, Reluctant Muse, Alice, Waiting for the Light, By Invitation Only, Picasso's Women, Enclosure, Lost Time*
POETRY EMERGING: *April Wind*
SLANT: *Leaving the Plaza, The Notebook*
TAPROOT: *My Literary Career*
TWILIGHT ENDING: *The Journey, Yes, The Veil, Last Hour*
VISIONS: *May Morning*

"Distances" was nominated for a Pushcart Prize.

My thanks to all the friends and cohorts, remarkable poets and authors in their own right, whom I've worked with over the years in various writers' groups, and without whose encouragement and "feedback" this book would not be possible. Special thanks to my daughter Jenna, a patient listener whose insightful comments have helped to shape many of these poems.

Table of Contents

PROLOGUE

A Visit from Calliope / 11

I.

Years Ago / 15
Exiles / 16
The Coat / 18
My Literary Career / 20
Cookie Cutters / 21
Haunted / 23

II.

Morphing / 31
Doppelganger / 32
She / 34
Pardon Me / 35
Turning / 37
Walking the Planck / 39
Patrons / 40
Myra's House / 42
Reluctant Muse / 44
Tiger / 45
Parade / 46

III.

Dreamscapes / 51
The Journey / 52
Connections / 53

Distances / 54
That Night / 56
Chores / 57
The Victorian Ladies / 59

IV.

The End of March / 63
April Wind / 64
Renewal / 65
May Morning / 66
Intruders / 67
Alice / 69
The Lake / 71
Autumn Pond / 73
Snow / 74
Yes / 76

V.

Visitor / 79
Bomb / 80
Deliverance / 81
Seers / 82
Kali of the Underground / 84
Stopover / 85
Strategies / 87
Generosity / 88
Royal Flush / 90
Ruminations of an Aging Feminist / 92
Waiting for the Light / 93
By Invitation Only / 94
Mona's Wedding / 96
Picasso's Women / 98
Structure / 100

VI.

Small Boat at Anchor / 103
The Veil / 104
Enclosure / 105
Letting Go / 106
Three A.M. / 107
Leaving the Plaza / 109
The Notebook / 110
Burnings / 111
The Gift / 112

VII.

The Catch / 115
The Swimmer / 117
Lost Time / 119
The Numbers / 120
Last Hour / 121
Seascape / 122
The Harvest / 123
Leather Thoughts / 124

ABOUT THE AUTHOR / 125

Prologue

A Visit from Calliope

It has been raining all week;
today the weather is cloudy but bright
like the brains of my best friends.
At this early hour
at this spotty kitchen table
wrapped in my old down coat
I sort out the contents of my soul.
I am pulling a long thread
out of my hapless brain.
Dried flakes of long discarded thoughts
fall to the floor unheeded.

I open the window: essence of dead possum,
soggy leaves brewing in yesterday's rain.
A cool breeze wafts through the untrimmed hedge.
Suddenly, there she is, bathed in morning mist,
gathering cans and bottles from the recycling bin.
She turns and winks at me. "Stuck again, Dearie?"
Long skirt trailing, stray leaves circling her brow,
she strides through the overgrown weeds to my back door.

Now she is laughing, leaning back in her chair,
feet on the kitchen table, munching on my last apple.
She sifts through a pile of old drafts,
nodding, gesturing, tossing unlikely phrases
over the griddle. My brain is sizzling.
I can hardly write fast enough.

After a while she takes her bundle,
ambles through the gate, disappears
in breaking sunlight.

I

Years Ago

we used to put cotton in our ears
when we went outside on a windy day.
Grandpa would be chopping wood,
a small drop of moisture trembling at the tip of his nose.

We took the little sled out to the pond,
where the sun glowed icy white
over the smooth green surface;
tiny things were sleeping in the plankton underneath.
On the far horizon, snowdrift and windswept clouds
merged to a vast infinity.

     * * *

The bed would be cold when I got into it,
Grandma's face bright pink from stoking the coal stove.
She would take a hot brick from the oven,
wrap it in newspaper, then in flannel cloth,
and place it under the covers, at my feet.
After she closed the door, the walls dissolved.
In the big mirror I could watch the moon
floating in gray-white mist.

Exiles

Long Island, 1940

Umberto sat with perfect military bearing,
wearing the old worn jacket, vest and tie,
thoughtfully fingering his gray moustache.
Lucia, little sister, leaned towards him,
one wrinkled elbow resting on the table.

"That much store cake," he intoned,
holding two bony fingers just an inch apart,
"*Veleno!* It makes me sick."
Lucia nodded, smiling her tragic smile.
They shared a delicate digestion.

Lucia's eyes were doe-like,
her left cheek dimpled, where a tooth
was missing; fine olive skin well prized
for eighty summers; pure white hair
bobbed in the fashion of twenty years before.

Through the long afternoon they sipped
the homemade elderberry wine
while the clock turned backward, backward…
Ships arrived at the Genoese harbor,
billowing full sail in the Mediterranean breeze.
Verdi wrote his operas.
The house where they were born
grew larger, grander as the day wore on.

Light filtered from the kitchen
where Albina rattled dishes,

or ran to wait on customers in the store.
No use asking for Umberto's help:
the "contessa" was visiting.

By three o'clock their childhood had run out:
he a young naval officer,
she an abandoned princess,
after that scoundrel from Palermo
lost her entire dowry in bad investments.

The elderberry wine was almost gone;
he fetched another jug. Glasses were raised
with long, aristocratic fingers
a little gnarled and swollen at the knuckle.
Their talk had quickened into Genoese.
They laughed at fifty-year-old jokes,
at stories of Uncle Silvio, long since dead.

Then it was evening. Grandchildren
chased each other through the house.
But we were only shadows.
The ship had not yet crossed the sea;
he and the young Albina had not met,
our parents still unborn,
and Mussolini only a nursling child.

The Coat

At age four, Sarah was the perfect hostess
in her pretty, well-ordered house,
clock on the mantel chiming the hours,
doorbell that made a little two-note tune.

Her mother was a kindergarten teacher.
She invited the other little girls over
for parties, taught us songs and games.
Here we go looby-loo, here we go looby-lie.

There was plenty of candy corn,
and Sarah greeted each guest at the door.
"Let me take your coat," she'd say,
and then the coat would disappear.

But that brown-and-white-checkered coat
was my favorite thing in the world!
Mother had to make it into a jacket
when it got too small for me.

I worried about it every time.
Who knows where she put it?
It was *my coat* and she took it away!
One day I had to take a stand.

She came at me, reaching for the coat.
I gave her a push, she fell backward,
sat down hard on the floor,
looking totally surprised.

I was pretty shocked myself,
couldn't believe what I'd just done.
I didn't mean to knock her down,
but there she was.

Oh boy, am I in trouble!
She's going to cry,
she's going to tell her mother.
They're all going to hate me!

But no. She got up, brushed herself off,
wagged her finger at me. "Now, Doris Mae,
you mustn't do that." She took the coat.
By then, I was glad to give it up.

We joined the other kids in the playroom.
Not a word was spoken about my crime.
My mother, who brought me, was the only witness,
and she, for once, was speechless.

What a relief! No tears,
no accusations, everything OK.
I knew I had a friend!

My Literary Career

My literary career
started early — a girl reporter
with a fashionably short skirt,
covering the waterfront, the shady
bars, hotels, laundry rooms,
my mother's kitchen,
anywhere news was breaking.
Then I would sit at my desk
and write it up on my toy typewriter,
breathing the sweet, pungent smell of the ink.
I published the newspaper
and read it all myself, from front to back.
The photos under the headlines
looked like people in the funny papers.
The women had to be very blonde,
or very dark, and have beautiful legs.
All the men carried guns.

Cookie Cutters

When I was ten, Mama put me to work
embroidering tiny flower petals
on identical linen towels, weaving stacks
of red and blue potholders, cutting dozens
of pale white identical sugar cookies.

Mrs. Davis didn't bake identical cookies,
never did anything the same way twice.
Her living room was cluttered
with colorful books and magazines,
bunches of flowers picked from the wild
overgrown bushes in her front yard.

Every morning the Davis cows walked slowly
across Route 25. All the traffic stopped.
In the evening they walked back.
This had nothing to do with Mrs. Davis
or the records she played — of Tosca
losing her beloved, of Violetta dying.

She was the only person in town,
besides the minister, who'd been to college.
Her walls were covered with pictures
of famous authors, historical figures,
prized horses, reproductions of famous paintings.
The other women thought she was "peculiar."

Mrs. Davis would talk for hours about her life
to anyone who'd listen.

Mr. Davis was not a listener.
He didn't talk very much, either.
If I were a cow, said Mrs. Davis,
I might get some attention.

If I were Mrs. Davis, I thought,
I'd sit up all night reading those books,
listening to those records,
and never cut another cookie.

Haunted

Sometimes she comes up and sits on her grave stone
(which is conveniently located on the back of my head)
and tells me I'm spending too much money on trifles,
like this seminar on goddess spirituality.
It infuriates her that she sat there cutting out coupons
for forty years to save money on beans and tomatoes
so I can spend $700 listening to actresses
talk about some goddess rising from the dead.
What sacrilege!
All night she mutters and rolls around in her dry bedding,
a thing I should not decently be contemplating,
but she tells me about it.

The year I went away to college
she insisted on selling the house — at a considerable loss,
because my brother and I had deserted her
and she hated the emptiness of the place.
Then she persuaded my father to go into business
with her sister's husband.
That was even more costly.
Still there was plenty of money left
to send me to the state school.
She was sure I would catch tuberculosis,
sitting in that big drafty library.

But I flourished,
like those ephemeral plants that live on air.
I continue to live on air.
It blows over the hills at midnight
and sends me swirling
among curious dreams and misty odors

to the strains of exotic music,
which is also air.

I tell myself I don't care whether she approves of me,
but of course I do. The guilt is terrible.
She follows me,
complains of her loneliness
and my criminal neglect.
I threaten nursing home.
She threatens disinheritance.
It's a very old script
from a play that never opened.
And now she's gone, and I am sixty-one,
living a strange, free existence I never knew before.

"The sleepless nights I spent, worrying over you" —
her voice gets higher —
"and now you're going to Hell
with people who don't believe in Jesus!"
I am hand-washing my purple blouses,
my bright red tee shirts, my black exercise outfits,
for the goddess seminar.
A dark stain spreads slowly through the water.
Then I scrub my sneakers, put them on the porch to dry,
and sit down to read.

She hovers in front of me, just at eye level,
tells me my windows are dirty,
that I'm straining my eyes.
I ought to eat red meat, and get myself another husband.
She never liked the first one, but I wouldn't listen.
My kitchen wallpaper has a smudge near the telephone;
there is dust under my bed.

She is working herself up, picking
at the DVD player with ghostly fingers.
Such a waste of money,
on a gadget she never even heard of!
And if I take one more expensive vacation
she is going to write my name
in the Book of the Damned
(I think she's bluffing about this one)
because God is good,
and He won't let my sins go unpunished.

I think about this as I pack my black tights in the suitcase,
along with a bibliography of the 26 books I've read
on goddess mythology, to share with the group,
and the poems I wrote for the women's spirituality magazines.
She won't read these, so I'm relatively safe.
But she might look at some of the pictures on the covers:
fat, naked goddesses; she-wolves howling at the moon;
two old women holding hands, smiling.
Much too happy.
She would be sure they were up to something,
the contemplation of which would make her shed silent tears
(always the most powerful weapon in her arsenal).

How could she have anticipated all this
when I was taking piano lessons
and singing in the Methodist choir?
She even sent my brother and me
to Bible camp one summer,
where people got prizes for reading
the *Book of John* over and over, for two weeks:
105 chapters, 214 chapters, 357 chapters.
My brother had his wallet stolen;

I nearly broke my back on one of their bikes.
It had no brakes.

All of which has nothing to do with my life now,
except when the seams of the house crack open a little
and the past creeps in,
with its eerie blue light and green feathers.
I bang my shin on the edge of the bed,
go stumbling into the kitchen for an ice pack.
Then her voice comes back.
And all the fancy knick knacks on my shelves,
that I haven't the heart to throw out,
look suddenly grimy and neglected.
I know she is lonely out there,
and I am wrong again.

"You should be mourning for me.
You should be crying your eyes out
and tearing your hair.
All I ever wanted was for you to be happy."

"How can I mourn for you, when you're *still here*?
You live inside my head. Every day we argue."
Now I am the one getting worked up.
"I am going to win this!" I shout at her.
"I'm going to live to be *one year older than you were!*
Then, when we meet up there,
you can't tell me what to do!"
Her voice comes back, imperious, trembling,
"I am still your mother!"

The sound trails away, the wail of a desperate child.
She is two years old again.

It's dark. She is afraid, and crying.
Her mother is somewhere in the apartment,
nursing her baby sister.
She screams. She beats her little fists against the wall.
Her father grabs her up,
puts her out into the pitch black tenement hallway,
and slams the door.

I am shaking.
I reach in the drawer of my nightstand
and take the Venus of Willendorf in my hand.
The cool clay figure gradually warms in my grasp.
I am connected to the earth.
I feel her pulse, which is my pulse,
throbbing in my palm.
She makes no rules, has no holy book.
Her silence fills the room.
She is the clay of my flesh. Of my mother's flesh.
The living and the dead.
My mother's breath is still in the room, but softer.
She is walking me to school on that first day.
We are holding hands.
Now we are kneeling
near the little pond behind the house.
She is digging dandelions for salad.
The smells of earth are all around us.
I can feel the sun on my bare arms and legs,
the cool grass on my bare feet.

God, how I miss her.

II

Morphing

In sleep I become a pile of wet leaves
heavy on the cold ground,
resisting the wind.

Sometimes I give up, let the wind scatter me.
Then memories fly in all directions,
my mind disappears, and I am no one.

I want to leave my memories behind,
like a fog that dissipates, bequeath
the contents of my head to someone else.

I could pass them to my cat,
who would blink and try to shake them off.
They might cause him to chase his tail endlessly.

Who knows what he dreams in his small brain,
what images pass before him?
I want to look through his eyes, feel through his skin.

Or yours. I want to live inside your head,
I'm tired of my own.
I want to be you.

Doppelganger

I have a monkey inside my skull.
He chatters and plucks at my brain,
pokes his dirty face against my eye sockets,
leers at the people outside.

He is strong — and supple.
He can roll my eyes where they're not supposed to look,
spit improprieties off the tip of my tongue,
his heel wedged against my jaw.

He smells bad.
I try to say polite words;
he tickles my throat,
belches his foul breath
between my teeth.

Sometimes he gets out and walks around the house,
picking up dust and discarded objects
between his ugly toes.
Inexcusable shit-colored beast,
he insults my work, laughs at the pictures on the wall,
exposes himself in front of my antique statuary.

When company comes I have to sedate him
and hide him under the couch.
Still he sticks out his fingers
and makes obscene gestures.
I pretend I don't see him.

I sip my tea and talk about books and art,
while he mumbles and drools on the floor.

Why couldn't I have a pet bird, or a kitten,
instead of this creature?

I'd miss him if he left.

She

shows up quite unexpectedly, leaning on the doorjamb
with a little half smile, smoking a cigarette,
as though she needs no introduction.

Pale speckled cheeks, hands paper-thin,
an abundance of unruly hair the color of charcoal.
Conversation will be useless. I let her in,
quickly retreat upstairs, pretending to have a toothache.

The house is confused, walls tilting at strange angles,
rooms misplaced, furniture receding into distant corners.
I seat myself before a large mirror
examining my pretend sore tooth.

All afternoon we waited for Aunt Emma.
I wanted to greet her in the old vestibule
with the carved wainscot, but that was long gone.
Her time of arrival was not at all clear,
or even whether she was coming or not.
Could this person be —? But Aunt would never smoke.
This woman is younger, her face, her body different.
Smoke from her cigarette is spreading through the house.

My daughter comes in, asking to rearrange her room.
Never mind that, I say.
Go talk to that woman downstairs.
Get her to put out that cigarette.

What woman? What cigarette?

I look in the mirror again. My hair is dark and smoky.
My skin is pale, black-spotted like a newsprint photo.
I stand up, stretch, walk slowly to the stairs.

Pardon Me

I meant to answer your call,
write that letter, but I'm
all tangled up in these
vines. It's not bad,
really. They have amazing
little leaves, and flowers;
they twine in a
friendly way.
It's just that they're
hard to un
tangle.
So I won't be able to
answer the phone
or respond to your message.
These things are getting
longer. They are lightly (not
unpleasantly) brushing my limbs.
Damn, now they're growing all over me.
I am a bank, a hummock;
water courses through my veins.
I smell like musk. Roots are sucking
into my arms like leeches, or the feet
of octopi. They can't get enough of me:
I have been elected president of my class.
I am the winner of the Miss America pageant.
I am loved.
The leaves are growing in my face, rustling in my ears.
The roots are tan, the exact color
of my legs. They are burrowing
into me. I don't know where I end
and this super plant begins.
I never fully appreciated soil before.

Now I *am* the soil; things grow on me.
I am a city of hungry gnats, a bank of earth
with a two-ton tree shoving its roots down my throat.
So OK, it's not that bad.
It's just these vines.
I'm tied up.
Sorry, you'll just have to wait.

Turning

I wish to be a mountain lion
in my next life. A lazy one.
To climb great heights, then pause
on a sun-drenched ledge, dreaming.
(Keep that in mind, God.)
A furry, lazy creature, capable
of great strength and sudden motion
at long-spaced intervals.

All day I have been writing letters
to people from past lives, in distant places.
My stationery is brown and tan,
rough-textured like old trees in winter,
the fur of wild animals.
Light streams in the open window,
mingled with musky odors.
My pen scratches over the page,
leaving a jagged trail.

Now the sun floats at eye level.
I stretch my limbs over the dark
green satiny sleeping bag
by the brick hearth.
Artemis the hunter looks on
from her high perch.

I dream of cool water, owls crying in the night,
foliage like blown hair, the drone of yellow bees.
(Remember that, God. Keep it in mind.

I have been very, very good.)
Long, lanky legs, restless twitching of tail,
sharp yellow eyes, blinking in sunlight.
A congenial pack of fellow felines,
supple-spined, heavy-pawed, willing to travel.
A wide, flat rock warming in the afternoon sun.
Keep it in mind. Just don't forget me, OK?

Walking the Planck

All the objects in this room are waiting
for you to leave so they can
fly out of place, reconstitute themselves
into waves of energy.

The little green plant with one red blossom
is leaning towards the wispy bamboo
shivering in its wet stones.
Wine glasses fidget behind glass doors.

The bird picture hangs a little off center,
a curtain bends longingly towards the open window.
They are waiting to come alive, like unruly kids
when the teacher steps out of the room.

Now they move only with permission,
like that ficus tree, swaying deliciously
when the breeze touches it,
now motionless, under your watchful eye.

So go away. Set it all free.
Objects will change to pure energy and back again.
Your whole world may replace itself
in a series of quantum leaps.

Don't inquire too closely.
Only a few can hear the music of the spheres,
the echoes from a parallel universe.
And we lock them up.

Patrons

No use insisting they are only crockery,
newly washed, rubbed dry with linen towels,
gleaming from terraced heights like patrons at the opera.
Stout sugar bowl with silver top knot,
tall stemware trailing its ribboned etchings,
round platter with its painted paisley waistcoat.

See how the burnished goblets
lift their rounded jowls behind the plates
bright-edged, stacked in multipetticoated splendor.
The piled cups lean, ears cocked;
plain glasses guard the slatted doors
like stalwart ushers.

They are the listeners.
They quiver when the trucks go by,
pulsate to heavy footsteps, taped symphonics,
or the unbalanced laundry in the old machine.
Wine glasses with their tinted cheeks
tingle together at the slightest movement.

Now we sit silent, I in my old cane chair,
they in their balconies of polished oak.
I muse and scribble at the disordered table
as they look on, bejewelled, impatient,
the soup tureen with elbows out in protest.
The crystal mugs shoot glances from the mezzanine.

Gift of an affluent uncle, long since gone,
perhaps too elegant for this plain setting.
He loved the arts; like him,
they wait in glowing expectation...

I feel compelled to stand, arms raised,
under the faded chandelier
and sing to them in quavery *bel canto*.

Myra's House

We were cleaning Myra's house.
It was the decent thing to do,
since we had all shown up unexpectedly
and she had that outside job.
There was grime everywhere,
dirty dishes under the TV stand,
and little Boo was feeling neglected.

We wanted to spread some joy that day.
Goodness knows, there's little enough
in Myra's life. Then suddenly
more people were arriving at the front door.
It seems there was a party planned
that Myra had forgotten all about.
She wanted to do it European style.
Guests were announced as they came in,
and something unique was said about each one.
We laughed and applauded,
felt we knew each other right away.

Every room was welcoming, even the bathroom.
It was large and had two doors with unreliable
hitch locks and a quantity of cheery pictures.
People kept opening those doors,
making friendly overtures.
I got out of there as fast as I could.

Long tables were set up for dinner.
Looked like the whole town had come to Myra's house.
Children were having a sled race outside.

Edwinna's little boy had lost his hat,
and we did what we could to cover him.

It was nice being friendly with Myra again,
after all those years of bile. I was glad I came,
even with all that housecleaning. We sat
at the table for a long time, reminiscing
while the others swirled around us
and danced in the costumes Edwinna had made
for them out of the curtains we took down.
We had pretty much dismantled Myra's house,
but she didn't seem to mind.

Reluctant Muse

Sometimes I wish I'd never met him,
but it's destiny, he tells me. His cat likes me.
What kind of guy lets his cat direct his social life?

I am curled up on the sofa, head propped
on a lumpy cushion, looking at one of his art books.
I roll to one side, trying to get comfortable.

Hold it! he says to me. Don't move a muscle!
I want to paint you just that way!

But—

No, no, just lie there, he says, go on reading.
He knows I can't eat anything in this position,
anyway, there's nothing in his refrigerator.

He has these excursions into the arts.
Last week he was learning to play the zither.
I sat there smiling, ear plugs under my headband.

Now the cat is walking all over me.
She's shy, and avoids most people.
I am one of her rare choices.

The cat is fluffy, has an even disposition.
As for him, he's moody, talks too much —
or says nothing for days.

I think the cat is tired of him.
Maybe I'll just sneak out of here
while he's cleaning his brushes,
and take her with me.

Tiger

There is a tiger loose in our community.
No telling where she will turn up.
Sometimes I think I hear her in the dark.
A twig snaps. Warm air is breathed into the night sky.
Her matted fur sweeps against the shingles by the back door.

What shall I do with a beast in my life?
I have enough trouble with the beasts inside my head.
I imagine her eyes, like fired kindling,
her nails like crescent moons
among the grass blades.

At night the damp earth exhales its odors.
A tiger prowls the neighborhood.
If you scratch her she will bleed
like any other creature.
But she has tough skin.

For weeks now they have pursued her
with their hounds and stun guns.
They see her in the dark, through telephoto lenses
but only now and then.
Today she entirely disappeared.

Parade

Mr. Bandmaster:
I will wait for your parade,
here on the pavement
under the unrelenting sun.
Legions of uniformed bodies
filling the city streets,
raging July colors unfurled,
thump of the marching feet.
Alleys and roadways blocked, roped off,
all journeys cease.

Mr. Policeman:
posturing, spreading your white-gloved hands,
sternly commanding the hapless crowd
as the spectacle begins.

I will wait —
for the beating of drums,
sounding of brass off key,
strut of the majorettes,
knee-high boots, white tassels flying,
sweating beneath their feathered hats,
doing their tricks.

The city stops
as the floats go by:
beauty queens with painted faces
sweetly wave while the old men laugh
and the flowers wilt in the noonday sun,
soda cans strewing the path.

They will skip to your tune:
young men, solemn-faced, awkward in khaki and brass,
old men stooped in their tight-fitting neckbands,
epaulettes drooped like aging peacocks,
limping under their weighted banners,
step to the pounding drums…

I will wait —
while the loudspeaker blurts commands,
Mr. Policeman clears the stands,
mayor and aldermen give their speeches:
voices metallic echo the hills,
as the microphone squeals in wild derision,
plied hyperbole fills the air.
This is their day, their time:
I will wait…

till the sun recedes,
and the crowd straggles by like dropped confetti,
popcorn bags are blown in the wind,
and the traffic slowly begins…

After they've gone I resume my journey,
cutting across the path they followed,
up to the hills by the gateway bridge
as the lights of the city blink on.

A free wind rises, swaying the trees
to a rhythm unheard, unplayed.

Mr. Bandmaster,
I never marched in your parade.

III

Dreamscapes

Try to remember every small detail,
the geography in which the dream unraveled,
the shapes of walls and how the light played on them,
whether these are people you have seen before
in different guises, or whether they are native to this dream.
These are things that no one could possibly explain,
and could easily escape the notice of Dr. Freud,
who thinks everyone in the dream is your father.

A dream may be inside or outside, with or without animals.
The setting may be round, like a castle tower.
Or it may be the tiny shop in which you bought
candles for last night's dinner.
Sometimes the sky completely disappears.

A dream can have its own peculiar music
which will stay in your mind for days —
an entire orchestra playing over your head
and only their feet are visible.
A passing car may sound like someone breathing.

Sometimes it is impossible to remember, upon awakening,
exactly where you are, because the world has changed
in the hour of your dreaming. And the place
where you've just been is so much more interesting:
a dungeon with smoke-stained walls,
an open scaffold over a thousand-foot drop,
a parallel universe where even the birds transmogrify.
You must wake up slowly from such a revelation,
or it could lose itself completely among your shoes
lying in the corner, the papers scattered by your bed.

Picture the room in which you fell asleep, then slowly enter it.
Your life may be changed forever, but no one has to know.

The Journey

Close the door gently;
do not look to shut me in.
I dream of clouds drifting
over endless fields
of very small flowers.
Sleep is its own dimension:
in this brief night
I live a thousand years
under the shadowed aura
of the sustaining moon.

Into the endless void
my soul seeks space
and time for wandering...
Lie down beside me:
stretch to the soft down pillows.
Let the mirrors of your eyes
reflect the colors
of your most secret places.

Connections

The train station is old, and cavernous
with a quantity of dusty ceiling lights.
The people sit half dozing, waiting to make their connections.
An ancient fan coughs warm city air into the room,
the smell of exhaust fumes, sweating bodies,
warm, salted pretzels, smoke stacks, rotting fruit.

The Chinese girl is young, and strong
with shining black hair and a colorful scarf.
She moves among the people, collecting fares,
selling picture books and rich, delicious cookies.
She has given me some very old Chinese money for change.

The people are anxious about their tickets,
about making their connections.
Everyone clamors to talk with the Chinese girl.
She is garrulous, but vague.
Chinese money is not acceptable to buy my ticket.
She smiles sympathetically and walks away.
Finally she agrees to take my check
but the check book has mysteriously disappeared.

The train is coming, out of the darkness
through the narrow tunnel.
My ticket costs forty dollars, but I have only twenty.
The rest is Chinese money.
I hold the paper notes in my hand.
They are covered with beautiful green etchings.
All the figures have a special meaning
which I cannot decipher.

Distances

Russia is very cold, very remote.
She touches Europe; she touches Asia.
But she doesn't belong to either of them.
Russia belongs to herself.

My friend Nadine thinks I should be more sociable.
You are like Russian winter, she says to me.
You have no lovers. I have three!
Why don't you come to the Boosters Club?
I am not much for boosting, I tell her.

Nadine's face is not beautiful
but she draws men to herself.
When she smiles, her plainness goes away.
Then she is bright; she is flawless.
But she is still Nadine.

She has more boyfriends than you! my mother says.
Look—she has three and you have zero.
Three is better than zero.
Why are you a zero?

Russia is sad, and far away.
She has impressive leaders in her history.
Often their names are strung out with epitaphs
like "the Great" or "the Terrible."

They rode fine horses. They played chess.
They were devoted to this large woman

whom they called their mother. They fought for her.
Then they ate her, piece by piece.

Today I went to the Boosters.
People were eating giant plates of food,
making noisy conversations on both sides of me.
I couldn't follow any of them.

I am a great tundra.
I am neither this nor that.
Nadine thinks I am a hopeless case.

THAT NIGHT

when she took off her robe
she discovered the awful
hollowness   a dark
blue space where
her belly
ought
to have
been
tiny stars
receding to a vast
infinity   the emptiness
of the universe   endless
void   nothing of her in any of it.

Chores

I really should have done something for Marielle,
she'd come such a long way to see me.
But she got here so early I had to put her
on a back burner, with all my other duties.

She was riding around town on a bicycle,
looking young and healthy, waiting for me to finish.
Marielle was always athletic.
She could have passed for thirty-five,
but everyone knew she was seventy-three.

I was driving from place to place,
taking care of obligations, in the old green
car that belonged to my mother-in-law.
I'd promised to take good care of it for the duration.

My last visit was to Cynthia.
I had trouble finding her apartment.
I was having trouble finding everything that day.
I parked the car in this vast garage
and when I came back, it was gone.

I kept walking through the place, looking
in the same nooks and crannies over and over
like a crazy person, even in spaces
much too small for an automobile.

That old green car was as big as a prehistoric turtle.
I couldn't stop looking.

Finally the garage man sat me down to tell me it was gone,
since I couldn't come to that conclusion on my own.

I'd walked before and I could walk again,
but how would my mother-in-law feel about this?
(She must be 100 years old by now.)
I'd have to get the police and report the car as stolen.

Just then Marielle came by again on her bicycle,
and I could see she was having a hard time.
It seemed she had lost one of her legs,
so riding that bike must have been a chore.

The prosthetic didn't fit very well,
was held in place by a giant magnet.
She'd gone for hip surgery, and somehow
her leg got transplanted onto another patient
by mistake. The doctor said he was really sorry;
he'd had a busy day and was multi-tasking,
a thing he didn't usually do.

My cell phone rang, and I knew
it would be my mother. She had just moved
into town and I hadn't seen her in years,
but the green car and Marielle's leg
were preying on my mind. I let it ring.

Maybe I could sue that nice garage man
for losing my mother-in-law's car.
It would be a start.

The Victorian Ladies

took their morning wash
from a simple bowl and pitcher
decorated with little rosettes,
spent leisurely afternoons
with their embroidery and three-volume novels,
took lengthy walks while listening to the birds.
Even maids found ample time to gossip,
slicing carrots, kneading the family bread.

They dressed elegantly in ribboned flounces,
loved passionately — mostly from afar,
wrote letters filled with shameless sentiment,
sighed over the flowery and prolific rhymes
of Mrs. Browning.

So have a Victorian day. Forget your shower.
Dust all the furniture — carefully, lovingly.
Re-read your Christmas cards,
sort them into little piles.
Write a long letter to a former lover,
sprinkle a drop of perfume by your signature.
Prepare a six-course meal from scratch.
Mend the hole in your stocking.
Have a friendly chat with the postman
when he arrives. Offer him tea.
Make a long romantic entry in your diary.

Don't watch the news.

And if you must go shopping,
take Lord Tennyson with you to the mall.

IV

The End of March

People are feeding the seagulls.
Feathers gray-white
as the late winter sky,
spindly legs set far apart
beneath their downy rumps,
they hobble along the lake shore,
snapping brittle offerings
in their arched beaks.

I jog along the sidewalk by an inlet
where two half-grown mallards
patiently navigate side by side:
a tan one and her colorful brother —
bright green, deep brown
in the luminous arch of his throat.
They stop to look at me,
decide I'm not too menacing,
go back to paddling.
The little male is cheating:
his feet are touching bottom.

The wind stings;
I pull up the hood of my winter jacket,
begin the long walk home.
A few tiny buds fight their way upward
through trash and gravel.

April Wind

blows through the hollow rooms;
white curtains move over empty walls.

Last night the rain, mixed with juniper seeds,
pounded your roof, my roof, with perfumed waters.

I watched from my window as your lights
flickered behind the wet branches.

Now the forsythia blooms are scattered on your lawn:
yellow shavings from the green god's face.

The willow stretches her pale blossomed arms,
the fingers lightly touching.

Dogwoods shake their white rag curls.
Tulips undo their yellow blouses.

Mornings, we will plant seedlings in perfect rows.
Evenings we will clip our separate hedges.

In May, blossoms will feather the front walk
like torn pillows.

Adonis will break out from his hollow tomb,
stretch his cold limbs, begin his dance.

Renewal

Glint of the afternoon sun
angles my windshield.
Down the familiar road
the trees drip pale green shoots,
soft tiny blossoms
white to pink to mauve…
On the far hills a haze of red berries
almost unreal in the fading light.

I open the car window,
feel the chill breeze,
hiss of the tires over the road still wet
from an afternoon shower.

Climbing higher, where the road narrows,
enclosed in an arch of greenery
clean, fragrant, beautiful,
as though the storms of winter never were:
millions of seeds ready to fall, spread, take root,
old weather-beaten branches
magically giving forth new buds,
gorgeous renewal.

Could I start my life over again?

May Morning

Last year's rowan berries, round dark clots,
cling to gnarled branches
under lush white petals.

Tiny stamens, soft as caterpillar hair,
nod over the shaded roadway
where small rivulets race down hill,
twigs and dead leaves washed
along the steaming pavement.

From this damp gloom,
a new mud turtle, neck outstretched,
raises on scratchy tiptoe
and begins to cross.

Intruders

In early May I find them,
along the walkway, underneath the porch —
fronds of wild carrot sprouting from the dust,
oak trees two inches tall, the acorns still attached.

I break my nails digging the crabgrass
at the edge of the parking lot,
in the long crack splitting the macadam
stuffed with green rushes like a giant fishmouth.

They fight back: small saplings cut red stripes
on my palms and fingers, a crumble of bloody leaves.
The tall ones line up at the edge of the blacktop,
waving their pennants in the wind.

Written in the curl of tiny roots,
cuneiform of the split seed, their memory:
lush primeval wood, fat snakes and possums,
beetles like fox eyes, black mossy streams,
the impenetrable green…

In June the heatherweed and Queen Anne's lace
blow their heady fumes.
They long to put us all to sleep
for just a century or two,
with all the engines rusting in the field,
sweet William, tiny buttercups
sprouting from broken hubcaps,

wild grass over the dirtblown roadway,
sunflowers over the plate glass windows at the mall.

They whisper in the dusk,
when the dank mist rises in yellow moonlight —
They want it back.
They want it all back.

Alice

Everything was happening
too fast; Alice was driving
recklessly, bracelets clacking
over the gear shift, wheels
skidding over the dirt road,
kicking up dust and gravel.
I could hardly breathe.

"We're going to be late anyway,"
I pleaded. Alice always took
the back roads, looking for shortcuts.
The old car sidled up the narrow path,
skirting a sharp cliff — looked like
somebody had dynamited the hillside.

I was trying to remember what we were late for,
why it had taken so long to get ready.
My lipstick had swollen, melted all over
like the strawberry ice cream cones
the kids were eating in the back seat.

Suddenly we went into reverse,
skidded to one side, barely missed
a large granite rock, then lurched
forward again. Alice's little girl and I
were clinging desperately to the bedpost.

Then she was gone. The air was heavy
with sweat and vaporizer fluid.

I opened the window;
a warm spring breeze drifted in.
Across the street, trees were dotted
with pale new leaves, curled and wrinkled
like tiny newborn hands.

The Lake

I

Our small canoe drifts over the surface
of sliced white mirrors, the broken shadows of birds,

through mud-washed water, past drowsy spotted turtles,
the shoals with their pungent weeds.

In the distance, a pale haze of new growth
scrumbles the hills like chest hair.

Below, the undulating weeds
gesture to no one in particular.

Small fish dart among slippery boulders,
moss, clots of green algae over the ribbed clay bottom.

A sunfish stares unblinking at our bubbly underside
where the waters open and close
open and close.

II

The land lies lush, recumbent,
like a great warrior sleeping,
a single orange feather in his hair.
Brown hills stretch lazily to water's edge
where a lone white swan waddles ashore,
shakes its glistening feathers.

III

The sun, like an old projector,
aims its cloudy lens at us,
spinning its reels to the click of flying insects.
We are the picture.
Our small prow, heading into the light,
appears to him as a serpent's face
nearly invisible,
its narrow little tongue a broken twig,
leaf stem, tail of a minnow.

Autumn Pond

Wild geese rise, splintering
the pond's pale surface
in honking crescendo.
A giant gander calls
from his brandywine throat,
dragging splayed yellow feet
through diamond-crested water.

Small mallards wake
from their summer torpor.
A white swan emerges,
slender and sun-struck,
from the dark brambles
on the opposite shore.

Gray-white gulls dip and glide
in the cooling wind, cast pale
shadows over thinning grass.
Children gather at water's edge,
toss crumbs like rose petals.

Snow

for Dorothy Towey

Frigid January morning,
I drag out of bed. All night
the fierce winds howled. NO WAY
would I budge from this warm cocoon
If I hadn't promised Dorothy.

Plows scraping outside —
four more inches overnight!
I am so tired of this blasted winter,
sick of this miserable *snow*!

Dig out the car, fingers
frozen under heavy gloves.
The engine sputters, and so do I,
all the way down the icy road
to Main Street, where I can barely park,
mountains of white stuff *everywhere*.

Dorothy makes her way
gingerly, over the lumpy sidewalk.
Now I feel *more* terrible,
couldn't even help her to the car!
Poor woman, over eighty years old,
how she must dread these miserable days.

She slides in, takes a deep breath…
"Oh!" she exclaims, "Isn't this — *beautiful*!"
I am lost for words.

Beautiful! she smiles, delighted, all the way out of town,
over the winding, drifted road to the secluded church.

I begin to notice how it swirls around fence posts,
clings to the trees with their prisms of icy twigs —
the whole white gorgeous landscape,
and the beautiful, delicate upturned face of Dorothy,
bright in the January sun.

Yes

We can hike
over a whited trail,
arms, thighs straining
over rock-strewn hills
under heavy back packs,
laughing in the wind's teeth.

Slowly we will savor the fish
caught in an icy mountain lake,
light candles at a small pine table,
amber light gilding faces,
our shadows merging
on the rough-hewn walls.

Later the curious moon
will pass white fingers over
abandoned plates, dropped shoes
warm rumpled sheets
lying like snow drifts.

V

Visitor

You are taking old boxes out of closets,
rearranging your life.
Now he is running for his.
Legs like tapered fingers,
faster than Chopin, faster than Liszt,
he races from the light.
So deft, so perfectly synchronized,
an alacrity you could never muster
(think how you staggered out of bed this morning).
But it's too late; you have spotted him.
Outraged, offended, you throw the book
you're holding, and he's caught.

He waits, trying to lose himself
between the darkness overhead,
the nubby strands of carpet underneath,
hoping you will forget him.
You lift the book and stare at him,
innocent filigree that he's become,
sunk in the heavy pile, unmoving,
a metal pin placed on a woven scarf,
a knurled design to frame a lady's watch.

And now he feels your grasp;
the rag of paper towel tightens around him:
the pinch, the small explosion, and he's gone —
small daub of paint on crumpled paper.
You shudder, toss the ball, try to forget him.

Bomb

We are sitting in a darkened room,
inert, like a drawing in charcoal.
A thief waits outside the window.
He swallows dreams, memories.

There is a bomb under the couch.
No one is trying to remove it.
We sip red wine, comment on
the inevitability of the explosion.

Then we stop talking about it altogether;
it becomes an impolite subject.
We play music, tell stories
to soothe our jangled nerves.

Today is the Official Celebration of Hope.
We wear bright colors,
pretend to love each other and the fate we share,
pretend safety, solidarity, high purpose

pretend we have time.

Deliverance

After the war, when the bodies are strewn topside,
when the pestilence has done with us,
the earth will give a little shudder of relief.

Grass will grow lush and vibrant green
over the cracked pavement, shattered brickwork,
archeological hub caps, radioactive car chassis,
charred fax machines, ruins of the opera house.

Giant horned beasts will return to the primeval plain.
Great, lavish serpents will emerge from the empty hollows,
churning the devastation into a rich, black loam.

Seers

After her children were murdered
by some ancient peacekeeping force,
Zeus thought that Lamia should have some
official recognition, so he gave her this gift:
he let her eyes see into the future.

Being clever, he made them removable,
said it would be all right on occasion to pluck them out
and loan them to friends or curious people.

Last Saturday I was waiting at the railway station.
Before saying goodbye my daughter whispered,
"Don't let that woman sit next to you; she's strange."

But she never looked at me, just nodded to sleep,
woolen hat pulled down over gaunt freckled cheeks;
she would suddenly open very bright eyes,
staring at some unseen presence.
Her hands, her head, were trembling.

At Grand Central I sat on my suitcase watching
casualties...mount... in...Middle...East...conflict...
more...troops...deployed...Dow...Jones...up...five...points
spelled out in green lights moving across the screen.

A woman in an old dusty coat
mounted steps, raised skinny arms, shouting,
"the burning times — your children — burning!"
Her voice echoed from the big dome
with painted constellations of the gods.

Stopover

At the roadside cafeteria
people are gathering into small queues,
fighting over the mediocre food.
"There, now!" a woman shouts at me,
"You've taken the last dish of Jello.
You have deprived my child!"
Little black hairs stand on her arms
like tiny shark's teeth.

I had been driving cross-country,
stopped for a quick swim before lunch.
Suddenly my clothes disappeared.
Wrapped in an oversized towel,
I joined the crowd at the lunch line.

"She's naked!" the woman says.

This woman has gone too far.
I elbow her out of my way,
nearly losing my towel in the process.
"The Jello is *mine*!" I snarl at her.
It is a bright electric green,
shining in the fluorescent light.
The cherry on top looks plastic,
the whipped cream fossilized,
but it's all mine!

After I eat, we resume our journey,
all my dead relatives and myself.
We are taking that trip to Yellowstone,

the one I refused to take in high school.
Wrapped in my towel, headlights blazing,
I pull onto the highway, barely missing
three crows fighting over a tasty roadkill.

Her eyes, like blinded moons,
shone through the tangles of her matted hair.

People stood in line, put down heavy luggage,
read half-folded newspapers, glanced at the clock overhead.
The New Haven train was running late, schedules disrupted.
Someone had thrown herself on the tracks
without warning or announcement.

If I had this gift, would I walk through the streets
in an old sweater and broken shoes
trying to give my eyes away?
Or step quietly in front of a speeding cab,
watching my own funeral?

Kali of the Underground

Inside she sits, dark goddess
wrapped in a brown tarpaulin,
all of her treasures held in a torn black bag
with broken handles,
glaring from glazed and heavy-lidded eyes
under her purple headband,
muttering at the empty seats around her.
This is her dwelling; we are intruders here.

The train reels through steel-girded blackness,
past shadowed figures etched on remote platforms
under bare bulbs.

Three young toughs grin at each other from the far end;
she spits them on the floor.
Scent of her anger hangs in the fetid air;
the people back away.
Kali the Destroyer,
working her jaws over some strange confection,
her teeth stained crimson.

We crash to a stop.
Unseen hands fling open the doors;
she watches the crowd push out.
I step over the void, glance sideways down the iron length,
its row of red lights like bleeding sentinels.

Upstairs in the pale gray afternoon
melting snow runs rivulets,
carrying things we thought we had discarded.
In the window of a novelty shop
a rubber heart writhes and beats.

STRATEGIES

You have great cheek bones — did I ever tell you that?
With your looks and my deviant brain,
we could conquer the world.
This house is too small for us,
this backwoods place doesn't do it.
The whole damn universe should be our playground.
We need to take flying lessons, learn a foreign language.
Did you save those Dominican quarters I gave you?
You gotta pay attention to these things.

Poor Allison's been waiting thirty years for her prince to come.
Those guys never show up when you need them.

Max has figured out a way to take over the neighborhood
by eminent domain. He keeps moving his garbage
closer to the neighbor's house and parking
old cars in their driveway.
He's a genius for acquiring things,
steals empty boxes and broken tools
from his uncle's machine shop.

Carla is coming tomorrow with her samples.
I suppose we'll have to listen to her spiel.
Family is family.
The cat is snoring again.
I let her sleep in my bed and she takes over.
They're territorial, you know.
We could learn something from her.
When was the last time you studied a map?

Listen, Margaret, we weren't made to rot around here.
We gotta have a plan, that's what.
Maybe that prince idea isn't so bad.
He might pick one of us.

Generosity

Monica always had a taste for antiques.
There she was, clambering up and down
my front steps and out to her car, her arms loaded
with lamps, end tables, whatever she could carry.

OK, I said she could have a couple of chairs.
I never liked that old stuff Aunt Aggie left
in my attic, but I had no idea there was so much.
And that girl wanted all of it.
I never saw her move so fast, wispy hair flying,
high heels cutting little holes in the front lawn.

She was piling up the back seat, the expandable trunk.
"Whoa! Who said you could take all that?"
It was more than just the attic —
half my living room was stacked on that car.
I could feel my mouth getting ugly. My lips were
spread out like a brass horn, teeth and gums flaring.

I was following her, panting to keep up.
The front lawn curved downward to the road
like a big field with overgrown trees:
my old school yard all over again,
where everybody robbed you —
your lunch money, your self respect.

My voice was reaching a scary pitch.
That furniture was looking shinier and shinier.
Suddenly it was gorgeous.
"I want it back!" I shouted. But she didn't flinch.

She slammed the car door, revved up the engine, left me
standing in a big cloud of exhaust.

Now the house is empty,
nothing but a few plant stands and that pesky cat.
And what will I tell Aunt Aggie when she comes to visit?
The place looks so much bigger now, with nothing in it.
The moon shines pretty on the polished floors.

Royal Flush

How did I know the duchess was outside the door?
She spies on me. We have been distant relatives
for years — the more distant, the better.

If the count shows up, shoot him.
He kills birds.
The night of the banquet, everyone dressed in feathers
to protest his murderous enterprise.
But he was not impressed
with the protest.
Things that rhyme don't interest him.
I wish I had half his chutzpah,
or a third of his retinue.
His men all dress in blue,
and when he makes his entrance,
they throw blue confetti, blue velvet balls,
and float a thousand indigo balloons.

Princess Anne was madly in love
with the servants — all of them at various times.
Her mum was furious. Each time she caught her,
she opened all the cages and let the dogs
chase her through the halls.

Wouldn't you like to take a walk around the grounds?
No, not those coffee grounds. They sprinkle them
in the corners to flaunt the evil eye.
It must be nice to have an evil eye.
I could look at my enemies and blast them in a twinkle.
That would depopulate the countryside, for sure.

Why are the royals so dysfunctional?
I blame it on the cards. The king takes precedence.
The queen has to choose between him and the knave,
the old father-son rivalry. And all the others
stand in sexless columns. How sad.
I think I'd like to be a ten. Ahead of all the others,
but out of the spotlight, standing just behind
the prince of the realm, where I can poke him
on ceremonious occasions.
But enough! The air is carbon free. Let's dance.

RUMINATIONS OF AN AGING FEMINIST

Maybe you're thinking about your lost love
or looking at that spot on the wall where you meant
to hang a picture, and suddenly you realize
you forgot to turn the page on your calendar —
another collection of wildebeests sent to you
by those conservation people.

Whatever happened to all those other calendars?
What year did you look at a new suffragette every month?
What about Georgia O'Keeffe and her suggestive flower petals?
The ancient goddess images, the dancing wiccans,
photos of the ERA march you did in '81?

    * * *

The lady on the TV screen is grim:
Men are being marginalized in the colleges.
Androphobic women are taking over the system.
Lady professors are forcing students to watch
The Vagina Monologues and other scary things on stage.
Conservatives everywhere are horrified
at what's happening in higher education.
And it's all your fault.

Isn't that refreshing?

WAITING FOR THE LIGHT

The gesture must always precede the words:
that's what they told us in acting class.
For example, you don't say "sit down"
and then jerk your hand out as an afterthought.
And if you say "how amusing" *before* you smile
this makes the entire statement insincere.

Hunger comes before a meal, and desire before sex.
And you must wait for the man to finish his speech
before you stand up and stretch,
especially if he pays your salary.

Even departures must be carefully timed.
Especially departures.
If I were to disappear, how long would it take
for them to worry about finding something
odorous and fearsome? We are destined
to become cadavers, after all.
The timing is everything. Just think
of the prominent politician who expired early
in the bedroom of an inappropriate woman
who was then faced with a disposal problem
of serious magnitude.

One act leads logically to the next;
everything must be preceded by the prerequisite other thing.
Eating the mousse before the roast beef is inexcusable
as consummating the marriage before the ceremony
used to be. The majorette struts *ahead* of the band;
the mayor comes by at the end, waving cheerily
from his decorated car.

And night must fall *before* the party begins
but only in the darker parts of the world.
In Swedish summer, anything is possible.

By Invitation Only

I was invited to the home of Morris Hokes,
script writer of a dozen memorable
high end films featuring albino apes
crashing through dark jungle undergrowth.

It was to be a formal dinner party,
"Black and white only," he insisted.
Morris had a tendency to literal mindedness.
It was the influence of those apes, I'm sure.

I arrived right on time, in white dinner gown,
black shoes, white gloves with tiny black fringes.
Morris was in his element, introduced himself as Maurice.
He was sipping a dry martini with the appropriate black olive,

had removed everything of color from his living room.
I thought I was taking part in a '30's movie.
(He had written a few of those as well,
claimed he had scripted some of the best silent films).

"Maurice" was speaking rapidly, gesturing
with his free hand. We didn't want to disappoint him,
but the crowd had moved outside, just to get some color.
We were beginning to feel like columns in a newspaper.

Dinner was served on the patio, boeuf noir with little white onions.
After this we were treated to a showing of his latest film,
which featured two white cats seated by a charcoal fire,
surrounded by acres of fresh snow.

They make purring sounds. One of them sneezes.
Suddenly the scene darkens, bats squeal
while flying over a stark white moon. The cats
make scratching noises. And then it's over.

"I wrote it myself," Morris explained,
"scripted the whole thing."
Everyone applauded.

Mona's Wedding

Mona got married last night. To Rich.
He just sort of showed up, very congenial,
and they spent time together — you know,
and things were going so well he said
Let's get married and she said Why not.

He must be a really resourceful guy, came up
with all the details in one day, the stuff
that usually takes months and drives you
crazy. He even bought her the gown,
a little off white, with shiny highlights,

a sort of one-size-fits-all. A lacy crown
topped it off. She looked in the mirror
and hardly knew herself, suddenly remembered
she'd been a pretty brunette, and her face
shone like the gown.

Rich took care of everything, invited
all his friends and his friends' friends. The room
was full of people she'd never met before,
all uniformly friendly and enthusiastic,
the kind that thoroughly enjoy a party.

She was glad she didn't know any of them.
The people she knew would have asked
a lot of nosy questions, and reminded her
of her last marriage, which had been
pretty much a disaster.

The dinner was the best part — lots of crêpes suzettes
and other soft, elegant foods that Mona enjoys,
especially as her teeth aren't so good anymore.
The room was elegant too: brass and mahogany,
a big stone hearth — the kind of place you could get lost in.

She couldn't seem to remember much
about the ceremony, or where they went afterwards.
Next day she was still snug in her old apartment,
wasn't sure where Rich had taken off to.

Her mother and father showed up, and she decided
she might as well tell them she was married again.
Mother was quite annoyed she hadn't been invited,
but the whole thing had been so spontaneous,
it wasn't really possible.

They were going on a trip, mother announced,
and leaving Grandma with Mona. It seemed
everybody was arranging Mona's calendar lately,
including Rich, who still hadn't turned up,
but she was sure he was out there somewhere.

Her day felt crispy and planned, as though
she finally had some structure in her life,
being married and all that, and she hoped
she'd be able to remember her new last name,
if they ever got around to asking.

Picasso's Women

"Les baigneuses," 1918

Placed in impossible poses
on a beach of dull green sand,
one leans her head to a vertical axis,
gazing at some unseen apex overhead,
her unwound hair trailing like sea grass.
Another, face averted,
sees only a distanced world behind the frame.
The third feigns sleep — or death? —
breathing the greenish atmosphere,
bending an elongated arm above her head,
pale elbow arched over the flattened palm.
(Pablo, this woman has two right hands!)

He likes to twist them, like clay images.
Torque interests him: thicken, and stretch.
Nobody has a neck like that —
was he thinking of horses?

The lighthouse watches them with its slit eyes.
Rows of wigged clouds float in a turquoise sky.
Rocks like warped marshmallows burgeon at their feet.
A sailboat juts from the flat, unwatery sea
like an empty claw.

Three women caught in suspended motion,
little round breasts like misplaced oranges
under their taut, unwrinkled suits
of fashionable colors — blue zebra stripes,

tomato aspic, hue of ripened eggplant,
circling their thighs. The zebra lady
is skewed in three directions
by an invisible hand.

Picasso's women — strangely mutated dolls.
How Gertrude must have loved them.
She always bought the ones that made her laugh.

Structure

First the floor gives
way, the founda
tion disinte
grates, I am
staring down a ten
story hollow cav
ern
etc.

The others are
having tea, and
it seems impolite to men
tion that the fur
niture is sliding
towards the edge of a prec
ipice or that the build
ing next door has
entirely disap
peared.

VI

Small Boat at Anchor

Her sail is furled, covered with sand
and the dung of passing seagulls,
the hatch swollen with too many rains.
The canvas cover lies on the deck,
cracked and broken.

My hands are stiff;
a cold wind catches my throat.
I kneel on the wobbly dock,
grasp the frayed rope;
the splintered hull draws slowly to the post.
Beyond the line of trees the sky glows
with the first streaks of yellow.

The Veil

Her body lies in a narrow boat,
dovetailed at bow and stern,
gliding ripples of blue and gold
from the receding shore…

Dry wisps of yellow hair, sealed eyelids,
fingers locked over white satin bodice,
bridal train neatly furled over slippered feet.

Ghost voices sound the hymn,
mingled with cries of birds,
while bronzed arms, muscled legs
guide through the cool water.

Dragonfly lights on her gathered sleeve,
draws together transparent wings,
balanced against the sway.
Flowers strewn on reflected shadows
follow her seaward course.

In the bedroom, morning stirs white lace curtains:
"Come here," he says. "I want you naked."
He moves, plays the familiar scene,
and never notices.

The wedding veil is thin, topped with a wreath of buds;
tiny white cups, pale leaves, surround that marble face,
veil gently rising in the wind…

Enclosure

The gates were always there
hard-shanked, muscular
cutting scars in the narrow pathway,
the arcs of opposing circles.
Beyond them we could see the fields
hollowed and yellow gold in the distance.

Then the sky closed in
painting its features on doors and windows.
A few giant rooks were blotted against the canopy
like smudges on a crinkled page.
Sometimes a sudden rain would envelop the dusty porch
like pounding waves.

Now the taste of our confinement
sours in the mouth,
flowers in the doorway
dry to stubborn little knots.

Fall is the burning time
the broken doppler of a passing train.

Inside, the floorboards creak and groan,
tables and chairs in disarray.
The dark spotted walls
are tinted with remnants of conversations:
an intricate paisley pattern
where a salamander suddenly appears.

Letting Go

It came to her in whispers,
leaves rustling under a graying sky.
The voices rose at unguarded moments,
more persistent as the weeks passed.

The house was in readiness, food prepared.
For weeks she'd kept the porch light on all night.
Dawns came slowly. Shadows retreated.
Wind cut strange shapes in the long grasses.

Late afternoons, a pair of mourning doves
crooned from a grove of trees, just out of sight.
She waited. The whispering grew louder.
Something had ended. There would be no return.

She went to the barn, opened the heavy doors.
His favorite horse, its black sides gleaming,
snorted impatiently. She raised the latch, watched
his tiny black figure disappear into the distant hills.

Three A.M.

I climb stairs, open the bedroom door,
switch the light on, then quickly off.
The sleeper stirs. I am a part of his dream.
I snatch the flashlight, disappear
into the silent hall and down the stairs,

put on my heavy jacket, boots,
turn the cool doorknob.
Outside, a powdery snow has been falling all night.
I watch, as millions of tiny flecks emerge
from black emptiness.

A cold wind enters me, my senses suddenly awake.
Beam of my flashlight forms strange patterns;
shadows bend and shift over white-decked trees.
I make my way up the deserted pathway —
hedges, lawns smothered in thick white mounds.

Stiff roadside bracken crackles under my boots.
My jeans squeak together like muffled shrieks.
A lone woman is stalking the night.
No one knows she is here. I am afraid of her.
But the night is so deliciously cold. I won't go back.

The road narrows among thickening woods;
my flashlight dims and falters; I shake it hard.
Its rattle echoes through the long tunnel of trees.
Small rustlings stir the underbrush.
The air is heavy with feral odors.

My light grows dimmer.
A quickened sound of footsteps,
a noise like heavy breathing.
A woman stalks the night. I follow blindly.
When I look up, the trees have disappeared.

And now there is nothing but the long descent to the lake.
Small points of light beckon from the other shore.
There is the rock marking the water's edge; there is the boat.
In a few weeks this black water will turn to frozen white.
I breathe great draughts of icy air; the night sky fills me.

At dawn the sleeper wakes, peers out his frosted window:
a light wind moves over the hillside drifts;
a thin veil spreads over the empty pathway, like white smoke.

Leaving the Plaza

A man is standing by the stairs
near the checkout desk.
His hair is red; he is thin, impatient.
He wears a tasteful three-piece suit,
a topcoat slung over his arm.
His eyes continually scan the lobby,
squinting, as over a vast expanse of sand.

Outside, the darkness rides on scattered leaves.
A stray cat, crouching near the side entrance
of the hotel, watches as I hurry to the curb,
my arms straining with heavy luggage.
A yellow cab slows to my signal;
we load suitcases, slam doors,
speed into heavy traffic.
A light rain spatters the dusty windows.

At the train station, I wait by the information desk.
The last night shuttle has already left.
Lights reflect on high, unreachable windows;
a loudspeaker echoes through hollow space.
On the wall is a giant map of the city.
I stand for a long time trying to decipher
its strange names, its random crossings.

At the hotel lobby a man stands by the stairs,
waiting. He is thin, impatient, hopeless.
I imagine him waiting there forever,
becoming part of the shiny surface of the wall
the dark marbled floor, the elevator, the night.

The Notebook

Scrawled on a back page, just one word — *Suzanne*
placed like a footnote, almost out of sight,
in my ex-husband's unmistakable hand

(the strokes I'd studiously learned to duplicate:
great phallic loops, descending with a flair,
to sign his checks, and see the bills got paid.)

How clever, how discreet, to hide her there,
for future reference, in the interstice:
just flip the empty vellums, she appears.

Mysterious coed? Someone else's wife?
I see a model's pose; rich auburn hair
cascades behind her ear. He'd find that nice.

Was she the legal wiz he hired last year
to fudge the income he forgot to claim?
Or femme fatale from his aborted stage career?

Perhaps a faithful, sweet-faced, willing slave,
paster of scrapbooks, booster of his fame,
juggler of schedules, finder of lost keys?

Or clever looks, beneath a shining mane,
her observations sharp, and polished well,
like the perfected sibilants of her name...

I don't know what about her caught his eye,
or why, at this late date, she rivets mine.
We have long since played out our history.

Hers was the only name I ever found.
I must confess: I hope she turned him down.

Burnings

I am watching smoke rise in tiny filaments
silent, unobtrusive as a book waiting to be read.

Light filters through the window
over the polished staircase, like blown candles.
Spoons glimmer on the unused linen cloth,
empty cups look on in amazement.

Evening was always a new beginning, a shared secret
as we waited for the sun's intrusive eye to disappear.
Now the waning light casts mottled shadows on the pane,
a strange geography.

All that we used to be, we have swallowed,
like Cronus, choking down the undigested bits.
Costumes, discarded masks, might betray us.
All this must be destroyed.

I stoop to my task
tossing the ribboned packets to the grate.
Smoke thickens, then slowly disappears.
How your words curl and blacken on the page.

The Gift

I saw him again last night.
So many years we'd gone our separate ways,
but still I knew him.

It was time for holiday, though the tree
was already taken down, or not up yet.
We greeted each other awkwardly.

The house was disordered, rooms half finished,
staircases rough hewn, with makeshift railings,
something we never quite moved into.

He lingered just a little while, then had to go
as ghosts and expatriates will do.
It would be my last chance to give him the gift.

The wrapping was worn thin, and falling open.
It was the thing I'd bought him years ago.
His pale eyes widened. He wanted it.

I hesitated. Why was I doing this?
He was a lost chapter, a forgotten scene.
I never re-read books or see films twice.

I placed the package in his hands;
he opened it. I looked away,
then suddenly he was gone.

In the morning, trees — old winter sticks —
were swaying in an April wind.
Buds sprouted from knobby twigs
like tiny cranberries.

VII

THE CATCH

I was watching at the upstairs window,
thinking of things I wished I'd said to him
and suddenly there he was, standing alone,
the moonlight catching at his hair.

I wasn't sure at first: his clothes were different
and he seemed so much thinner.
He stood there looking up
as though he wanted something.

The moon was so bright
I could see his lower teeth,
the pale border inside his lip,
his eyes looking past me.

You remember that hat he used to wear
with the visor, the cloth-covered button on top.
He came back to get it.
I don't know how I knew.

I opened the window, held it out to him.
He crouched a little, like a catcher, waiting.
His eyes were very bright
as though everything depended on that moment.

I aimed it carefully; it weighed nothing.
He watched as it careened toward him,
a terrible concentration
that seemed to take all the energy left in him,

reached out one ragged arm, caught it,
then turned and walked away
with that peculiar limping gait of his.
It would not have occurred to him to ask for more.

The grass was blue white
in the unshadowed, empty yard.
He didn't turn, or look at me, or say a word.
Then he was gone.

The Swimmer

The sea is cold, and steel gray.
The rocks are hard under your feet
but you hardly notice them.
Closer in to the surf, there is sand.
Your legs tremble in the wind; your bones ache.

She is someone you had coffee with,
who happened to sit on the stool next to yours.
Someone whose name you didn't memorize.
She looks like your older cousin,
high cheek bones, red hair slightly askew.

The salty wind tastes like blood in your throat.
Still she insists on swimming, though it's late in the day.
You watch her plunge into the surging water.
A small crowd has gathered at the food concession.
You try to explain that you never met her before.

Now she is calling your name.
She is not on the surface,
or the line where the waves break.
You strain your eyes in the opaque glare.
You plead for help, but no one hears you.

Far out are the reefs, the jagged rocks.
A wooden crate floats by, sharp-edged and broken.
Still she calls your name.
You imagine her floating underneath somewhere,
her suit the color of waves.

You stand in the freezing water.
Her voice is everywhere.
The people at the concession stand are frozen in time.
You look for the place where she entered.
The sand holds no footprints

The undertow tugs at your feet; it's getting dark.
The body of a man rolls in on a giant wave.
No one seems to notice.
He is stiff, in a seated position.
You cannot see his face.

You try to remember her conversation, her history.
She seemed to come from nowhere.
How cold, how motionless, that man rides the waves.
How they seem a part of him.

The cries have stopped.
Another man is washed ashore.
His hair is iron-gray, and thin.
He is bent like something strung with wires.

Would you have plunged into that icy water
if you had seen her, just glimpsed her?
Would she have pulled you under?
You walk away, and no one calls your name.

Lost Time

This morning on the digital rowing machine
I could hear the simulated slosh of oars,
the imaginary rowers locked in symmetry.
You are three boats behind… you are seven boats behind…
you are much too late…
All day the people flex their muscled legs, climb
virtual steps, trek endless rubber roadways,
ride bicycles to nowhere.

Tonight my bedroom clock counts out the seconds,
rearranging its red lines in perfect measure.
Something is hitting the window pane in little ticks:
tiny white crystals glitter on the pavement, the grass,
the rough, broken edges of the roadway.

Years ago my grandmother walked out of time
to a garden lush with buzzing cicadas, the odor of oleander.
When the fever left, she came back.

The train to Albuquerque is very expensive
or I would have gone a long time ago
but I don't suppose I'd find you.

The Numbers

I must get rid of the numbers —
I cannot keep them in my head any more.
I will pile them like leaves on the front walk;
people will have to step around them.

I have counted the birds, the trees,
the snow flakes, the diamonds in your hair.
I have counted the miles, the seasons,
all the years we've lost.

If I could have you with me, just for a day,
we could scatter them in the wind
or spread them on the lake
to float downstream.

We could watch the sun rise over the canyon,
listen to countless birds,
make up for all the time we've lost
and drown the ledgers.

Who will save the willows when we can no longer
count them, or measure drops of rain?
The numbers are stacked in dry heaps
and the wind refuses to take them.

Last Hour

The trees are bare on top,
nodding and whispering like a row of old men,
a little brown and yellow hanging about their ears.

All day the light makes subtle overtures;
at the last hour it goes mad
flailing the hillside with its fiery pink undergarments.

How long have we waited here?
When it's all over, will the color eat itself up?

How you hid from me all those days,
how I made smoke screens to blur the wanting of you
that spread in me like a chain of infinite windows.

Now we watch the colors disappear like snowmelt
or an unopened letter burning.

Seascape

Fog, gray mist, cold slippery rocks, pale green lichen
clinging to the weatherbeaten dock,
washed in the tidewaters.

Night comes earlier now, before the season's change.
Summer lovers, we walk the familiar shoreline,
bobbing together like driftwood.

Yesterday the sun rose like a burning disc,
amber reflecting on wet sand,
a scene from Mars.

Now the rain sends shivers through our backs,
our suntanned legs. A puzzled moon
squints through the opaque sky.
Gulls cry and circle in the cool salt air.

A wave crashes, spreads its white foam over the shore,
pulls wildly back down the long slope, tearing sand
from under our feet.

I want to stay here, be a part of the gnarled seascape,
weeds, sand catching the crashing surf, the part of you
that touches me, and then
pulls back.

The Harvest

for my father

The summer's past and will not come again,
the seed pods fallen and the weeds grown tall.
My turn has come to tend the orchard now,
take tenderly the speckled fruit in hand,
and turn the soil along the tangled paths.
My spade is lighter but will have to do.

Through many seasons your deft hands
would prune these trees, trim the once-perfect rows
where wild unruly grass begins.
You were the giant of these well-kept fields,
and I the princess, running barefoot
down enormous leafy aisles.

Now with weathered hands
grasping a useless hoe,
you gaze bewildered
while the last blaze of sun
filters through veined leaves,
at the ripe hazy globes you cannot gather.

I'll carry the familiar baskets home;
and when the chill of autumn settles in,
clasp hands, and lead you gently from the gate.
And we will sit together by the hearthstone one more time
when that cold wind begins,
when the harvest is done.

Leather Thoughts

We could take the train…
hoist our bundles up the metal stairs,
ride backward in worn leather seats,
watching the snow flakes glance off smoky windows.

Huddled together, feet propped on suitcases,
plotting our route like happy fugitives,
I would lean close to catch your words,
breathing the earth scent of your warm jacket.

Riding the long anonymous miles,
swaying with every stop,
your gloves would lie on the seat next to mine,
the fingers gently closing.

About the Author

Doris Henderson grew up in a very small town on rural Long Island. She attended the State University of New York at Albany and holds an M.A. in English and Comparative Literature from Columbia University. A former teacher and theatre coach, she sees poetry as a performance art. Her work has been published in many journals and anthologies, as well as three chapbooks: *Transformations, Leaving the Plaza,* and *Distances.* Doris lives in Danbury, Connecticut, where she attends workshops with writer friends, does freelance editing, and serves as president of the Danbury chapter of the Connecticut Poetry Society. She has four children, six grandchildren and a cat named Azure.

This book is set in Garamond Premier Pro, which originated in 1988 when type-designer Robert Slimbach visited the Plantin-Moretus Museum in Antwerp, Belgium, to study its collection of Claude Garamond's metal punches and typefaces. During the mid-1500's, Garamond—a Parisian punch-cutter—produced a refined array of book types that combined an unprecedented degree of balance and elegance, for centuries standing as the pinnacle of beauty and practicality in type-founding. Slimbach has created an entirely new interpretation based on Garamond's designs and on comparable italics cut by Robert Granjon, Garamond's contemporary.

To order additional copies of this book
or other Antrim House titles, contact the publisher at

Antrim House
21 Goodrich Rd., Simsbury, CT 06070
860.217.0023, AntrimHouse@comcast.net
or the house website (www.AntrimHouseBooks.com).

•

On the house website
are sample poems, upcoming events,
and a "seminar room" featuring supplemental notes,
reviews, images, poems, discussion topics,
and writing suggestions offered by
Antrim House poets.